How To Deal With Difficult People

By Madison Taylor

Table of Contents

Chapter 1: Introduction

You probably have dealt with difficult people ample times throughout your life. Difficult people are inevitable. Unfortunately, this inevitability is very hurtful. Nothing can ruin your day like a difficult person. Difficult people are able to make you doubt yourself and your efforts, while presenting you with intense hurdles that you must jump over.

You probably deal with difficult people in your work, your family, and even your social group. Whether you deal with a difficult boss or customers every day at work or you deal with people who hurt you in your family, you are probably bombarded with people who seem to be out to get you. These people say hurtful things to you, or they refuse to work with you. You find life to be more challenging because of their influences.

Don't let difficult people ruin your day. Difficult people usually have personal problems that they take out on you. It is not your problem that they are so hard to get along with and that they are so unpleasant to be around. Sadly, you may take many people too seriously. It is time to remove the seriousness from difficult situations so that you can enjoy your life.

You also need to learn how to move past difficult people. It is possible to work around difficult naysayers in your life and get your way. It is also possible to persuade difficult people to get along with you and work with you better.

There are many ways that you can undermine the difficulties that difficult people create in your life.

It is possible to find ways to work with difficult people more easily. It is also possible to condition yourself to stop taking difficult people so personally. This book offers you ample tips on how to minimize the damage that these difficult people cause you.

Chapter 2: Different Types of Difficult People

There are many different types of difficult people that you may run into during your life. Understanding these people can help you understand how to deal with these people in the best way. Understanding the fundamentals of what makes difficult people act the way that they do can help you find ways to work around the difficulties that these people pose for you.

When Difficult People are Your Fault

You first must understand the fact that what you need or want is not the same as what others need or want. When you experience conflict between your goals and someone else's, you may perceive the other person as being difficult. In reality, he or she is not necessarily a difficult person.

It is important to become more empathetic and patient. Just because someone does not want the same things that you do does not mean that he or she is a bad person. Sometimes, it is really you being difficult because you refuse to bend. Understanding when you are being difficult is important. You can determine when you are hurting others and you can change your behavior so that you are more flexible.

Flexibility is crucial when you are trying to work with other people. You are not the only person in the universe. While you are entitled to your own preferences and desires, you are not entitled to always getting your way with other people. Sometimes, you have to accept the fact that what you want is not best for everyone involved. When you are working with other people, sometimes a compromise or other arrangement is necessary.

When it seems that everyone in your life is difficult, you may want to reevaluate the situation. Is everyone being difficult? Or are you being hard-headed? You are probably the common denominator when everyone seems to be working against you. It is time for you to make some sort of change.

Stop blaming other people for being difficult all of the time. Start to consider that you need to bend and be a little flexible. Things cannot always go exactly your way. Accept that other people have different needs and desires than you and will fight you for things that go against their beliefs or needs.

Communication is key in this situation. You should clearly communicate what you need. Then find out what other people need. Make people feel needed and valued by listening to them and focusing on their input. Once you do that, you have the grounds to begin making progress with the "difficult people" in your life. Whether that progress involves reaching a mutual solution or compromising, you can achieve it when you facilitate decent communication.

Dramatic

There are certain people in your life who will prefer pitching a fit than just working with you toward a goal. These people lower the quality of your life by adding drama and stress to it. You cannot seem to work with such people. You even come to fear them and hate them because of the stress and turmoil that they cause.

It is important to understand that dramatic people are running a form of manipulation on you. Much like small children pitching violent temper tantrums over candy in the middle of the grocery store, these people have learned that overreacting will get them what they want. They are used to bulldozing their way through people's barriers by acting like babies. If you take a close look at how dramatic people act, you will find many similarities with babies, actually.

Dramatic people will be difficult to you in many ways. They will overreact to everything. They will spread rumors about you and start fights with you. They will steal the spotlight from you all the time. No matter what they do, they will lower the quality of your life with their dramatic antics.

Rude

Rude people are great at just ruining your day. By being rude to you, they let you know that your feelings have no relevance to them. They make you feel worthless and less than human. You often wish you could just be rude to these people right back, but often you cannot, especially if you are encountering these rude people at work. Customer service is an example of a job where you must fake a smile and tolerate rudeness. Dealing with family sometimes calls for you to endure the rudeness of overbearing family members, who don't care when you confront them.

The most important thing is to be empathetic and to not take things personally. Rude people are usually rude because of their own issues, not because they hate you. Try to be understanding and you will find that the rudeness hurts a little less. You can also try being rude right back and setting up boundaries with these types of difficult people.

Stubborn

A stubborn person poses the ultimate hitch in all of your plans. Stubborn people refuse to give you a break or let you have any leeway.

You must do what they want and you stand no chance to get your way.

A mixture of flexibility, teamwork, and persuasion can do wonders in making stubborn people budge. You want to be empathetic and you want to work with a stubborn person toward some sort of mutual goal. You also want to convince a stubborn person to give up his or her ego in favor of what you want. You can only accomplish this by using persuasion and great communication. Cultivate a sense of teamwork.

Uncertain

These are the people who drive you crazy with their uncertainty. These are "maybe people," who never have a clear yes or no answer. Their fickleness and unsureness make them difficult to be around and difficult to work with. You want to scream, "Make up your damn mind!" but you can't. If you work in sales or on teams, you probably deal with people like this all of the time. While it is infuriating, you cannot rush or pressure an uncertain person.

Instead, you can use persuasion to sway and convince uncertain people. You can also offer negative consequences to fickle people so that they will stop changing their minds on you. Be fickle right back or cut a fickle person out of your life to stop flaky behavior.

Insecure

Everyone has some type of insecurity. Insecurities are a natural facet of human nature. Humans often find comfort in locating their own faults because the human brain is programmed to focus more on the negative than the positive. But excessively insecure people can be very difficult because they do not believe in themselves at all. They are riddled with trust issues and they say terrible things about themselves. You may find it hurtful to see how much these insecure people suffer. Or you may just think that they are annoying and looking for attention.

Whatever reason that an insecure person proves to be difficult for you to contend with, you have to use some empathy and try not to take his or her insecurities personally. He or she probably suffers a great deal and does not mean to be so annoying. In addition, he or she probably needs some tenderness and love. If you simply cannot stand being around an insecure person, then consider cutting ties or offering tough love to teach the insecure person to be stronger. You do not have to enable insecure behavior by offering a person comfort and compliments all of the time. An insecure person who is starving for attention will quickly snap out of it if you react with tough love. Just be careful not to break a truly insecure person's heart by being too tough.

People who are Never Happy

We all know that one whiny, pessimistic person. This person always whines and complains, to the point where it appears he or she just loves being miserable. He or she asks us for advice but disregards it in order to stay unhappy. There are ways this person could fix his or her problems, but he or she staunchly refuses to do anything.

Understand that this person is just in a negative place. It is not your duty to console, comfort, or advise this negative person. Just put distance or tune out his or her negative words. Stay positive. You do not need such bad forces in your life.

Sneaky and Underhanded

Sneaky people are hard to deal with. This is because you do not know what their real intentions are or what they are really doing. They do things you do not want without your knowledge. They work to undermine your authority, as well.

This sneakiness is not nice. It can be very frustrating. It can also make you question your relationship with this person, as he or she has proved to not be trustworthy. How can you manage such a person? The answer is complex. You must use a combination of deflection, persuasion, and negative consequences to make such people respect your boundaries.

People You Love

This may seem like a joke. But think about it. Probably the people who pose the biggest challenges in your life are the people whom you love the most. Your love and the fact that you spend a lot of time around these people make them so difficult. You constantly worry about your family and friends, and you fight for them. You are annoyed by their personality flaws and quirks but you also love them. Loved ones can be the most difficult because they know that they can get away with it.

Good communication can help you resolve almost all differences with loved ones. Your loved ones are likely to lie, fight, and rebel to keep their own freedom. Try not to be over controlling. Instead, be understanding.

Chapter 3: Why People are Difficult

Causes of Conflict

There are many reasons why conflicts arise between you and other people. These conflicts are what make people so difficult. Often, you get along with someone just fine until your needs or views start to conflict. Then, you realize that this person poses a hardship or hurdle of some sort for you. You must understand the cause of conflict in order to go about solving these conflicts. Once you solve conflicts, you will find that a majority of difficult people suddenly become easier to deal with.

Four Intents

There are four intents that commonly lead to conflict. These intents are where you may run into difficulties when dealing with other people.

The first intent is to get a task done. You want to get something done. Other people may or may not care about getting it done. You can run into some conflict trying to get other people to focus on working with you to get a task done.

The second intent is to get the task done right. People are apt to have their own ideas about how everything should be done. As a result, you will run into a lot of disagreement on how to get a task done right.

The third intent is to get along with people. Most people share this intent in theory. But when it comes to practice, many people have no clue to all get along. People all have different needs and communication styles. This can make getting along difficult as everyone conflicts.

The fourth and final intent is to earn the appreciation and recognition of others for your efforts. You are likely to run into a lot of conflict here. Not everyone is going to appreciate you or your work. If they do, they may express their appreciation in odd ways. Some people may be jealous of you or angry with you, so they refuse to acknowledge something that you have done well. Similarly, you may make others resentful when you do not provide the recognition that they desire. Lack of recognition is likely to create a lot of conflict.

Lack of Communication

A lack of communication is the most common root of conflict. If someone becomes difficult, you are probably not communicating well. You both get frustrated as you misinterpret each other. You get insulted over things that were not intended to be insulting, you develop groundless expectations, and you create delays and discord. Clear communication is essential to resolving conflict. I will cover clear communication tips later in Chapter 5.

Differences

Different ideals can make you not get along well with a person. You may have different ideals about lifestyle, work, religion, philosophy, or ethics. You may have different goals in life that do not mix together well. Whenever you experience a difference of preference or opinion with someone, you face the possibility of conflict.

It is important to be understanding that other people are not the same as you. Be sensitive to differences in backgrounds, cultures, and opinions. You should let go of conflicts where you are trying to change or convince someone to see things your way. This is just not a reasonable or useful endeavor. You will probably just wind up frustrated.

It is also important to stick to your own guns. You have the right to lead life as you see fit, and you should be firm in your decisions. You do not have to explain yourself or lie about yourself, you just have to be firm and resolute. Your firmness will end a lot of the meddling. When it doesn't, you can politely ask them to leave you be and stop trying to deviate you from your goals.

Fear

Fear is a common cause of conflict. People will fight you if they feel that you pose any sort of danger to them. The danger does not have to be a physical threat. If you threaten someone's comfort and routine, you can stir up a vicious reaction. People are fiercely defensive of their comfort and will refuse to work with you if you pose a threat to their normal way of life or of doing things.

If you bring change with you, you will scare people. People will become difficult as they fight to maintain their routines. Try showing people how change will benefit them so that they become more accepting of the tides of change that you bring. Sometimes, you should just not try to fix something that is not broken. In other words, if the change you bring is not truly necessary, why expend so much effort to force it on people who do not welcome it? Consider that you might be the cause of peoples' difficult behavior if you are trying to force useless change on others.

Pride

A cause of most conflict is probably pride. Pride lies at the bottom of stubborn and difficult behavior. People refuse to bend to you because of pride, so they act in difficult ways. You may also engage in pride and refuse to bend as well. As a result, everyone behaves in a difficult way and nothing is accomplished.

Pride can be a useful emotion. But it is best in small, healthy doses. Recognize when your pride is getting you nowhere. Drop your pride in favor of a good solution. When it comes to others' pride, try to avoid hurting their pride and offer them lots of benefits for working with you.

Reasons People Act Difficult

If someone is particularly challenging, you might want to consider why. It is always a good idea to be empathetic in all areas of life. By being empathetic, you can pinpoint and thus address the cause of someone's difficult behavior. You can find some sort of solution that works out well for everyone. There are many different reasons for why people act in difficult ways, beyond the causes of conflict that I discussed above.

Consider these different reasons if you are running into problems with someone.

Bad Day

People can be difficult or rude when they are having a bad day. Consider that people who snap at you or treat you badly may just be at their wits' end. They may be tired, hungry, and crabby so they are not willing to be nice and easygoing. A person who does not feel well for health or emotional reasons will probably be difficult.

Try to be more sympathetic and understanding. Do not take someone's random outbursts of rudeness or difficult behavior personally. It is likely unrelated to you. Usually, when someone acts out, it is for their own personal reasons. You can try to communicate and ask them what is wrong, or you can just ignore the behavior and move on with your life.

Unintentional Rudeness

A lot of the time, people do not intend to be rude. For whatever reason, someone may act rudely without even meaning to be rude. Try not to take rudeness so personally and understand that there may be legitimate reasons behind this rude behavior. Do not let someone's behavior determine who that person is for you. People often are not their behavior.

Rudeness may be bred out of habit. People who have been raised in rude families or who have not been reprimanded for their rude behavior before may continue to act rudely without even realizing how hurtful their behavior is. These people will often be shocked and even confused when confronted.

It can be caused by cultural differences. These differences may be as small as regional cultural differences. Someone may be rude to you because he or she is simply acting in a way that is normal to his or her native culture. Some cultures do not believe in smiling, for instance. Other cultures may be brusque or may be open to asking what Americans deem as invasive questions. If someone is not from your area, consider that a cultural difference is at play.

Disabilities can also lead to rudeness. Some people suffer from social anxiety and are not able to follow conventional social rules in public because they are so nervous. They are desperate to get away from you and may not respond to things that you say or may appear to avoid you. People suffering from Asperger's or other disorders on the autism spectrum are also unable to follow conventional social norms. If someone acts oddly around you, do not become offended or confront them. Instead, consider that something is wrong. Not all disorders are starkly visible to the naked eye, so reserve judgment and hurt.

Then it is perfectly possible that someone is simply unaware that he or she is being rude. People who are in a hurry or preoccupied with something else may inadvertently treat you rudely. People who have not been taught any better while growing up may also act out in rude ways, without intending any harm.

When someone is rude, consider that he or she did not mean to be. You do not have to get all upset over someone's rudeness. Stop wasting so much emotional energy on people that have little importance in your life. Their lack of manners may have been unintentional. Even if they mean to be rude, you do not have to let it affect your day.

Lack of Respect

Deliberate rudeness, deceit, manipulation, and underhandedness all serve as glaring signs that someone has no respect for you. People who disrespect you will not take you seriously. They will not mind hurting you and violating your boundaries. The difficulties that they pose for you are bred out of their lack of caring for your well-being.

When you realize that someone disrespects you, you can either walk away or present someone with consequences for his or her disrespectful treatment of you. Do not tolerate disrespect. Offer a serious punishment to those who do not treat you right. Sometimes the best punishment is to withdraw your affection and leave the scene.

Opposing Views

A person who views something differently from you will pose a huge difficulty for you. He or she will work to erect boundaries in order to satisfy his or her own goals and block yours. He or she may also try to tell you what to do and change your course of action or your beliefs.

You can work with such people by offering a compromise. Discuss your opposing views and make it clear that you are not interested in changing yourself or the other person. Agree to disagree. This is impossible for some people, so walk away from such people.

Insecurities and Jealousy

Insecure people tend to get jealous. And jealous people are often hateful. A jealous person will be the worst enemy that you ever have. He or she will constantly work to hurt, undermine, and discredit you. His or her goal in life will be to bring you down, so he or she deliberately targets you all of the time. A jealous person will pose many difficulties for you.

Jealousy often arises when someone is threatened by you and perceives that you possess something he or she wishes to have. Whether this is success, a romantic partner, looks, money, or a valued possession, you will encounter difficulties deliberately created by this person. You can identify people who envy you by their unexplained, intense hatred and their apparent obsession with ruining your life.

Deal with envy maturely. Take it as a compliment. Then try to communicate with someone who is jealous of you with great kindness. Tell him or her how to get whatever you have that is so coveted. You can kill this kind of difficulty with kindness.

Revenge

Vindictiveness also can make a person become difficult for you to deal with. Someone who has it out for you will prove to be a formidable enemy. Consider if you have made any enemies somehow. Is there a reason that this person may hate you? Do you two have prior history?

If you find that someone may desire revenge on you, then apologize for your wrongdoing and offer a reasonable solution. Try to make things right. Prove your innocence if you did nothing wrong. Open communication is often the best solution to this issue.

Chapter 4: Don't Take it Personally

Part of the reason that difficult people create so much trouble is because you tend to take their behavior personally. If you think that people are difficult as a deliberate affront to you and if you take difficult behavior as a sign that people do not like you, you will spend a lot of your life very hurt. The key to dealing with difficult people is to stop taking their behavior so personally.

You need to realize that people are acting out for reasons that are most likely totally unrelated to you. It may be any one of the reasons that I listed above. It may be a completely different reason that no one else knows. But it is probably not directly because of you. Only in rare circumstances is someone's difficult behavior ever targeted at you.

When you stop taking things too personally, you stop stressing yourself out over the behavior of others. You can start the process of nullifying or balancing out others' difficult behavior. There are many things that you can do instead of becoming upset or angry about difficulties with other people. What are some of the things that you should do instead of taking things personally? Take a more constructive approach to difficult people, rather than a hurt and personal approach, so that you can transform difficult interactions into more rewarding ones.

View Difficult People as a Challenge

Do you want to know what sets successful salespeople and entrepreneurs apart from average people? It is all in the attitude. Successful people are far more likely to view difficult people and situations as fun challenges. They welcome difficult people and make it a point to "win" with difficult people. They do not take things personally or give up in despair.

It is important to start viewing difficult people this way yourself. Think about how this is a great opportunity for you to turn someone's attitude around. Focus on bettering the situation, rather than running from it or worsening it.

Empathize

Having empathy makes life so much easier for everyone. As you become empathetic, you become able to understand why people do the things that they do. You become more gentle and caring. You avoid a lot of misunderstandings. It becomes easier to forgive people for their transgressions when you understand what they were feeling when they performed an action.

Try to look at things from someone else's shoes before you rush into any judgments. Changing your perspective is the key to empathy. Consider their recent life circumstances and their personalities. Consider that you may have triggered them to have a certain reaction. Consider how prepared they may be to handle situations well. If you try to view something through someone else's eyes, you may realize someone's motivation and reasons for acting in certain ways.

For example, someone who has endured an abusive childhood will probably not have the best coping skills for relationship problems. When you two fight, he completely shuts down and stonewalls you. Instead of taking it personally and thinking that he must simply hate you, try to consider how difficult it is for him to handle relationship stress. Give him another chance and communicate your needs with him. "I understand that you hate fighting. But I hate it when you shut down. Can you please talk to me instead of shutting me out?" is something that you could say to this individual.

Try to Find the Source of Difficulty

It is better to be proactive and to approach life from a solution-oriented angle. When someone is being difficult, just drowning in your sense of upset is useless. Rather, it is far more conducive to success if you try to fix the situation. Exploring why someone is being difficult can help you find solutions to their behavior.

You can start by facilitating open communication. Have you ever tried asking a difficult person what is upsetting him or her? Try it and you might be surprised how much he or she will soften. People are not used to having others care. If you appear to care, people will often soften toward you and work with you. They will realize that you are not so bad after all.

Find a Balance

Understand that it isn't your Fault

A major part of not taking things personally is to understand that most of what other people do is not your fault. People have their own problems. They spend most of their time wrapped up in their own issues, so that they have trouble understanding how their behavior affects others. While this is no excuse for rudeness, it clears you of fault when people act difficultly around you.

Some people are also very selfish. They are so focused on their own goals that they neglect to think of your own sanctity and happiness. Don't blame yourself for being weak. Blame them for being terrible to you. You should be more assertive in the future, but do not beat yourself up for being kind and trusting.

Don't Define People

It is easy to judge people based off of their actions. We are often taught to put more value in actions rather than words, and for good reason. The actions of others often speaks volumes louder than their words. However, when someone exhibits some difficult behavior, you might want to reserve judgment for later. People are not always defined by their behavior.

It is common to think, "He is such an asshole" or "She is such a bitch" after observing less-than-desirable behavior in someone. But you should never make such assumptions right away. You should give someone a second chance before you label them and shut them out forever. You may find a great co-worker or best friend in someone, so don't write someone off based on a brief observation. Would you want someone to forever think badly of you just because you had a bad day and acted abysmally once?

Observe someone over time before you make a judgment. Do not base your judgments of someone's character off of one incident. Instead, look at their general demeanor over several incidents.

Avoid Drama

You have a few options when you encounter a difficult person. One option is to silently suffer. Another option is to blow things up and start a fight and a lot of drama. Drama is stressful and it will burn bridges between you and other people. Drama is always best avoided.

It is usually best to appear better than others with your behavior. That way, you will appear reliable and mature and you will not be blamed for anything that happened during a difficult exchange with someone else. Maintain your innocence by being an emotionally detached observer. Do not engage in drama if you want to avoid further problems.

You have a real chance of working things out with someone if you behave in a non-dramatic manner. But if you behave in a dramatic way, you are likely to alienate someone and obliterate all chances of working issues out.

Don't Let It Affect You

Do not let the behavior of other people change who you are. When someone is being difficult, it is human nature for you to want to change. You harden your heart, you become angry, you want to lash out at people. Your moods and your personality can change in the face of opposition.

But understand that the behavior of others actually has very little bearing on your life. Most people who bother you with their rudeness or underhandedness are not actually important in the long run. Ask yourself, *Will this person's behavior even matter to me in a year?* If the answer is no, then you should not let this person affect you so dramatically. Do not change for him or her. Do not let his or her temporary shenanigans have permanent implications on your life.

Make like rubber and make them glue. Let their words bounce right off of you.

Chapter 5: Play More Nicely

When dealing with a difficult person, you usually feel like you are alone. You are standing on one side of a fence, and he or she is standing on the other side. It may seem practically impossible to hop the fence and work out differences. However, you would be surprised how much easier difficult interactions with people become when you extend your hand metaphorically and try to work with them as a team.

There are many different ways to work with people to resolve difficult situations and conflicts. Sometimes, just talking about it helps. Communication is always essential for conflict resolution. Becoming a better communicator is crucial to removing the blockages that prevent easy human interaction. The keys to good communication are nestled in this chapter.

Facilitate a Team Effort

Facilitating a team effort is when you make it appear like you are actively working with someone on a solution. You are a pair, or a team. But how can you invoke this feeling in people?

The first step is to have a solution-oriented attitude. Show this to others by asking questions like, "How can I make this better?" Really show your interest in reaching a solution. By expressing this interest to the other person, you are basically extending an offer of help while inviting him or her to join you in the endeavor.

The second step is to actively make an effort to accomplish a reasonable solution with someone. You can't just say you want to help and then not help. This is an actual effort that you must make. When the other person sees you making this effort, he or she will more than likely jump in as well. Actively talk or search for a solution to the problem that is causing someone to be difficult to you.

It is important to not be overbearing in this endeavor. This is not all about you. It is also about the other person. Focus on him or her and what he or she says. Do not become bossy, or you will just cause yet more resentment and conflict.

Be open to things like compromise. Also be open to using persuasion, which is covered in more depth in Chapter 7. A difficult person is a puzzle that you must do anything to peacefully work around and placate. You must open yourself up to a wide variety of solutions and never give up until you find the best one.

"We" speech is helpful in teamwork. Say a lot of "we" terms to make the other person feel like he or she is included in your thinking. This will subconsciously trigger someone to feel like you are on the same team. In fact, it can be helpful to use "we" terms right off the bat with anyone to create a cooperative teamwork bond from the start. A lot of friction can be shed if you approach people like teammates and try to work with them, instead of against them.

It is perfectly acceptable to want to be superior at times. Especially if you are very knowledgeable in a certain field or subject, you can be superior. But understand that having a condescending attitude is a surefire way to alienate other people. People will not like you or want to work with you if you appear to be a know-it-all. Instead, have an open mind and accept new information. Even if you already know everything about something, smile and thank people for their expertise. You will find that people will respect you much more if you do not tout your infinite knowledge all of the time.

You also should never be accusing when you are trying to work with people. It is easy and natural to become resentful of certain people. You may want to say things like, "Because of you, this happened" or "Thanks for ruining my day." But it is important to not hold this attitude if you want to avoid further conflict. Instead, dissolve your resentment with a sense of humor. Do not level accusations or unkind statements at other people, or they will just get defensive. Say that you do not like the conflict and that you want to work things out. Never implicate someone's fault in any situation, no matter how big or how small.

People also tend to love solid, basic ideas and plain language. Making things less complicated is a good way to open communication with other people. Try to end conflict and make someone feel included in your efforts by eliminating confusing or unnecessarily fancy communication from your dialogue. While big words are a sign of intelligence, people will actually appreciate it if you use simpler language. They will feel like you are trying your best to be clear and direct, which will make them feel like a part of the team.

Finally, never be afraid to take the lead. Every team needs a leader, even if it is just a two-person team trying to overcome a conflict. If you are trying to create a conflict resolution team of some sort with at least one other person, you can appoint yourself the leader by taking the initiative. If you do not take this initiative, then the other person probably will not either. You two will get nowhere as a result. Do not be afraid to be the bigger person and start the team effort on your own. Other people will respect this and follow your lead.

Communicate Better

You already saw how important communication is for dealing with difficult people. I have mentioned opening good communication in almost every section of this book for good reason. A great deal of difficult situations with people arise over misunderstandings and poor communication. Having great communication skills can also help you resolve conflicts with people by searching out and targeting their needs and making it clear that you want to help, not fight. You would be surprised at how much difficult people will soften and work with you when you begin practicing good communication skills.

Many people believe that they are great communicators. They blame difficult situations and miscommunication on circumstances or other people, not themselves. But if you are running into difficult people frequently, you may want to reevaluate your communication skills. Let's put it this way. You can never be too good at communicating with other people.

NLP Tips for Great Communication

Neuro-linguistic programming (NLP) is basically a philosophy or lifestyle that teaches you to use the neurological, linguistic, and physical attributes of yourself or other people to achieve your ideal results. While it can be used for a plethora of means, possibly the most beneficial aspect of NLP is learning how to communicate most effectively with other people.

Intentions

In order to be a great communicator, you need to set a very clear intention for your communication. If you do not understand your own intention, then your listener certainly won't. You want to know exactly what you want to communicate. You also need to know your desired outcome for an interaction. For example, if you are confronting a very difficult co-worker about her obnoxious and unfeeling behavior, you need to set some intentions and desired outcomes for the confrontation. You may want to set the intention of helping this co-worker adjust her behavior so that you get along better with her. You may also want to express your feelings, which she has hurt. Your desired outcome is having a more peaceful and less hurtful relationship with this co-worker, so that you can complete your job without wanting to strangle her or to lock yourself in the restroom and cry.

Plan out conversations with difficult people before you initiate the conversation in reality. Envision how you want the conversation to go. Imagine how the person you are talking to will respond to you. Make a goal for what you want to achieve with the communication. The more you do this, the clearer your communication will become. You can avoid pesky misunderstandings because you do not make the mistake of being unintentionally vague.

Sensory Acuity

NLP believes that all people have a preferred sensory acuity, or perceptive sense. Some people prefer auditory, while others prefer visual, and yet others prefer gustatory, olfactory, or tactile. You can gather clues about what sensory acuity people prefer from their speech. A tactile person will say stuff like, "I love how that feels" and "Do you feel what I'm saying?" A more visual person will utter phrases like, "Do you see what I mean?" and "That looks really nice." Auditory people will refer to hearing, olfactory people to smell, and gustatory people to taste.

Now it is very important to find someone's sensory preference because you can use that information to facilitate smoother communication. People will respond to you better if you use their preferred sensory acuity when you speak to them. For instance, if you are an auditory person but you gather that a person that you are talking to is more visual, start using visual references in your speech, such as, "Do you see what I am saying?"

Matching

Matching is another NLP tip for getting people to communicate well with you. Match someone's breathing to give him or her a sense of being close to you. Matching your breathing rate to that of a difficult person can make him or her suddenly like you and respond to you better.

Matching facial expressions and body movements is also helpful. People find comfort in similarity. They will like you more if you seem similar to them.

Finding common ground with someone is also helpful. Imagine that you are dealing with a very difficult customer who is shouting at your co-workers. You can instantly appease her temper by pointing out that you like her earrings and you have a similar pair yourself that you wear often. Or if a difficult family member likes a certain sport, try to get into the sport with him. Watch how quickly people simmer down when they see that you share common interests with them.

Tonality

There is a lot more to communication than just words. In the next section, I will talk about body language. But tonality is also a big part of communication. Tonality is how you phrase words and the tone and volume of voice that you use. In fact, an estimated thirty-eight percent of communication lies in how you say things. It isn't what you say, it's how you say it.

Use more positive terms when you are dealing with a pessimistic or doubtful person. For instance, describe a car as "fast, efficient, and attractive." Don't say things like, "That car won't leave you stranded on the side of the road." Even though that statement may seem positive, it is really negative because you are talking about a potential negative event. Avoid bringing up negative events or using terms like "won't," "don't," and "can't."

Also use subtler language. Instead of using strong words like "steal," use the more lax word "take." This lessens the drama and seriousness of the conversation for others, so that they feel more comfortable talking to you.

Keep the volume of your voice reasonable. Never raise your voice when dealing with a difficult person, or you will probably set yourself up for communication failure. Use a gentler, more soothing voice when dealing with upset people to calm them down. You can raise the intonation at the end of sentences if you want to appear more approachable. Alternatively, you can lower your voice if you want to appear more competent and intelligent.

Body Language

The nonverbal aspects of communication account for fifty-five percent of your communication. The way you posture your body as you speak tells others a lot that you do not say. Conversely, you can gather a lot of information from how others posture and carry themselves as they speak to you. You need to be very aware and mindful of your own physiology, as well as others'.

You want to be as open as possible when you talk to other people, particularly difficult people. Around rude or unpleasant people, you naturally will desire to cross your arms and brace yourself against them. But it is better to have a relaxed, neutral posture when you speak to others. Relax your arms at your sides and lower your shoulders.

Eye contact is also crucial. You do not want to stare into someone's eyes during normal conversation or conflict resolution, but you also do not want to avoid making eye contact. Eye contact lets others know that you are sincere and that you can be trusted. Relax and try to meet someone's eyes often.

When dealing with difficult people, you may find that mirroring is helpful. This is when you mimic some of the motions that someone makes while talking. If someone leans toward you, you can take a brief three-second pause and then lean toward him or her as well. Mirroring makes others like you more since they recognize similarities in you.

You should always have a confident posture, with your shoulders back, spine straight, and head held high. This posture lets others know that you cannot be bullied. It also lets them know that you are a knowledgeable and authoritative person, so they will want to listen to you. Managers are usually great at adopting this posture and using firm language to settle disputes with unhappy or inappropriate customers. Model your behavior after these managers and do not ever give in.

Behavior Patterns

People communicate a lot with their physiology and tonality. Observe and interact with behavior patterns that other people exhibit during communication. When you do this, you become more sensitive to what others are saying without speaking out loud. People will appreciate it when you pick up on their subtle cues, without forcing them to speak about something directly. Speaking directly can be awkward and even rude, so do not force people to spell things out for you. Gather and respond to their behavioral hints before they have to say something out loud.

Watch for external shifts in behavior when you are communicating. Facial expressions may change ever so slightly. Someone may cross his or her arms in defensiveness, or may shift slightly toward an exit, indicating discomfort. When someone's cheeks flush, he or she is feeling more heated emotion and getting more excited. When you notice a change in someone's tonality or volume of voice, you can surmise that his or her emotions have changed and a topic is important to him or her.

Always respond to someone's behavioral patterns during communication. Not doing so can make you seem stubborn, insensitive, careless, or even unintelligent. If someone tries to express emotion through behavior, try your best to placate negative emotions and encourage positive emotions. Offer your coat if someone shivers or offer to talk somewhere else if someone shifts subtly toward the exit. Read customers to gauge their concerns about the products or services that you are selling. Doing these little things can make a world of difference because it makes others feel like you actually care.

Chapter 6: Reflect Difficult Behavior Back

A risky but effective way to deal with difficult people is to give them a taste of their own medicine. Some difficult people do not realize how awful they are being toward you. Showing them their own behavior can help them realize that they need to make an attitude adjustment. Other people do not care if they cause you emotional harm or strife, but they will hate having their own behavior reflected back to them. They will probably leave you alone after tasting their own medicine.

You do not have to tolerate anything. When someone is being difficult, you may have the best luck trying to resolve the conflict using the tips in the previous two chapters. But you are certainly not required to always work with difficult people. You have the right to shut difficult people down when they try to add strife and hardship to your life. You may sometimes have the best luck being difficult right back to people. In addition, you may enjoy a cathartic release from putting someone through the same obstacles that he or she put you through.

Often, reflecting someone's difficult behavior right back to him or her will teach him or her a valuable lesson. No one likes to experience pain. When you hurt someone in the same way that he or she hurt you, he or she will not enjoy it. Some people will recognize that you did to them what they did to you, and they will grow regretful. They will adjust their behavior as an apology to you. You will teach them a very valuable lesson that they will probably never forget.

A great example of this is when you find that someone repeatedly manipulates and lies to you. Doing the same thing right back can be very helpful in teaching manipulators and liars how much their behavior hurts. Manipulate manipulative people. If you catch someone trying to manipulate you, you can put on a smile and reverse the behavior. For instance, if your romantic partner is being difficult and tries to pout to get you to leave a party that you wanted to go to, you can pull the same pouting act at an event that he or she makes you attend. If your spouse texts you and says that he or she will be working late, but you know that is a lie, you can say that you are working late as well and let him or her catch you in the same lie that he or she told.

When you are being manipulated, the genuinely best reaction is usually to do exactly opposite of what your manipulator wanted. Let's go back to our example of the manipulative partner who pouts to get out of social events. When you see this partner start to sulk and try to ruin the party for you so that you go home, do the opposite. Ignore your partner's childish behavior and start having a great time. Manipulators hate being thwarted and they will learn to try different antics if their usual ones stop working on you.

In customer service, it can be beneficial to lose all friendliness when dealing with rude customers. You can reflect unfriendliness back to people who are rude to you in any situation, but this method is especially great for customer service because it is discreet. While you should not be blatantly rude because of the conventions of polite society, especially in customer service, you can often show rude people how awful they are being by dropping your usual friendly demeanor and becoming stone cold instead.

Say someone walks into your department store and refuses to acknowledge your pleasant smile and cheery greeting. After looking around for a while, the customer decided to start berating you for not having the particular product that she is looking for. You do not have to maintain your extremely cheerful demeanor. You also do not have to be rude enough that you get fired. Strike a happy middle ground by losing your smile and becoming more unfriendly and professional. You are able to seem more respectable and you are able to reflect your displeasure to rude customers by doing this. I have had great success using this method in customer service. Some customers do not care if you are hurt by their rudeness, but most customers are just having bad days and will stop being rude when they see how much they have irritated or hurt you.

It can also be a blast to engage in verbal jousting with difficult people. This method is certainly useful in deterring mean co-workers or family, especially at events such as Thanksgiving. Your rude and querulous family members who have no boundaries and say whatever they want to you will be very surprised when you show up at next Thanksgiving full of equally insulting comebacks. People will be shocked that you have the audacity to speak to them the way that they speak to you. They will more than likely feel stung and back off from picking on you. In the future, they will fear your tongue and they will avoid making their usual ugly comments.

Fickle people are a waste of your time. They disrespect you by never giving you clear answers. You can reflect this behavior back on fickle people by not showing up. Be just as flaky back. Most fickle people will forget about you when you stop responding, and they will cease to be a burden on your precious time and resources. Others may realize how annoying and hurtful fickleness is, and they will change their ways.

You can definitely change a pessimist's tune by being extremely optimistic. Let your positivity outshine their rainy day parade. Refuse to let them drag you down.

A final great way to shut down deliberately difficult people is by remaining cool, calm, and unaffected by their behavior. Often, people try to get a reaction out of you. This reaction satisfies their cravings for attention or lets them know that they have succeeded in hurting your feelings. Do not take the bait and let difficult people provoke you. If someone is frequently able to draw you into a nasty argument, surprise him or her by suddenly just not responding to any provocations one day.

There is often power in silence. You can definitely freak people out by refusing to give in to their petty jabs and attempts at hurting you. You will be the stronger person, and you will emerge on top in the power struggle.

It is entirely up to you if you want to get revenge on difficult people in your life. But if you do decide to be vindictive, do not feel guilty. You are getting cathartic release while teaching difficult people to respect you. However, keep in mind that these methods may backfire. Often, walking away or trying to reach an agreeable solution is the best option when dealing with difficult people.

Chapter 7: Persuasion

Persuasion can help you get ahead with people who are stubborn or dead-set against what you want. You can persuade people to want the same things that you want so that they will become willing to work with you. You can convince others to share your intents, thus eliminating conflict and difficulty. Persuasion gets people to say yes to you without a fight. Powerful persuasion methods are outlined within this chapter. Use them to get your way with any difficult naysayers in your life.

Have a Purpose

When you try to run persuasion on people, you want to have a clear purpose. How will this benefit you? How will it benefit the person that you are trying to persuade? Is it really worth the whole effort of persuasion? Outlining all of the benefits and uses of your proposal can really help you find out how to sell it to others. Try to root out what will make something appealing to other people, and then sell your proposal on that.

Appear Selfless

You cannot persuade people to support your interests if you make it all about yourself. No one wants to do something just for you. People usually are out to serve their own interests. Therefore, you want to appear selfless when you are trying to persuade someone about something. Instead of talking about how something will benefit you, focus on how something will benefit the person that you are trying to persuade. Really sell the idea or product or proposal to the other person. Leave yourself entirely out of the conversation.

It helps to find out what other people really want. If you know what someone wants, you can spin a proposal to directly appeal to him or her. The more accurate and personal your proposals are, the more likely others will buy into them and say yes.

Ingratiate Yourself

Using the rule of reciprocity, you can ingratiate yourself with people by doing them lots of favors. Human beings are naturally inclined to want to pay back favors and services that they have received. If you repeatedly put yourself out for someone by doing him or her favors, you can cause him or her to feel guilty and to want to reciprocate your kindness. You can put a lot of people in your debt and then use guilt to get them to pay up when you need a favor.

Be an Authority

One of the most difficult situations that you can find yourself in is a disagreement about an issue. You may run into family members, co-workers, and even friends who hold entirely different political views or lifestyle values from you. Your differences in opinion and perspective can lead to arguments. How can you persuade someone to come around to your point of view?

It is never guaranteed that you can persuade someone to share your particular beliefs. Often, it is not even worth the effort to change someone's stance on an issue. You can agree to disagree with far better consequences. However, appearing to be an authority and projecting maturity can certainly help you win your case if you want to pursue challenging someone's beliefs. While you should not expect any miracles, you should certainly try to present your case in the most calm and rational way possible. Speak in a smooth voice and articulate your ideas in a steadfast, intelligent manner. Do not ever admit to doubt; appear totally confident and unwavering in your beliefs. Do not raise your voice at any point. Maintain eye contact and a confident posture. If you present an argument in this manner, your confidence will suggest that you are an authority and it may persuade weaker people.

You should also employ Aristotle's wisdom of pathos, ethos, and logos. Pathos is someone's emotionality. You want to appeal to someone's emotions by making your point seem agreeable. Ethos is your credibility. You want to seem like you know what you are talking about. Logos is logic. Your argument needs to make logical sense or it is bunk and no one will buy it. Use these three things when you try to argue a point and present yourself as an authority.

However, not everyone will be persuaded. You should not waste too much time or energy arguing with stubborn people. You will get nowhere and you will fight for no good reason.

Framing

Framing is a very powerful tool that can be used for persuasion and manipulation. When you frame something, you place it in a context that makes it seem appealing to someone. You create an atmosphere that induces a person to want to say yes to whatever you are proposing.

Here is a simple example. You want to eat pizza, but your friend keeps bringing up Chinese. You can expose your friend to the smell of pizza, or else you can keep talking about how delicious pizza is all day. By dinnertime, your friend's mind is now framed on pizza. You are probably going to both agree on dropping by your local pizzeria instead of the Chinese buffet.

Yes Framing

You can frame speech to get people to want to say yes. You do this by creating a yes frame. A yes frame is when you ask a series of questions with obvious yes answers. For instance, you might ask, "You love your kids, right?" and "It's a nice day, isn't it?" The more yes questions you ask, the more likely someone is to keep saying yes. Then, when you pop the big question, such as "Do you want to buy this car?" the person is already predisposed to say yes.

Foot in the Door

Difficult people can put a serious hitch in your plans when they refuse to do what you want. You can get difficult people to feel more inclined to do what you want if you use the foot in the door technique. In this technique, you start asking a difficult person to do a series of very small favors for you. These favors need to be simple and convenient for the difficult person. The person is likely to agree to do these small things for you. This puts him or her in the frame of mind where he or she wants to do things for you. Then you can ask for a bigger favor, and you are more likely to get a yes.

For instance, your dad might be difficult about lending you his car. You can start to ask him for little favors, like money to go to the candy store. Then ask him for a ride. Finally, ask him to let you borrow the car. He may want to say yes after doing you favors all day. He will be eager to be rid of you for a little while.

Door in the Face

Door in the face is the literal opposite of foot in the door. When you employ the door in the face method, you ask someone a ridiculous favor, something so huge that they are practically guaranteed to say no. Then, you ask for a smaller favor. Someone will probably say yes since the smaller favor seems reasonable compared to the huge favor that you first asked. You basically want to get people to shut the door in your face in exasperation, then relieve them by asking for a much smaller favor.

Create Urgency

When you give someone a sense of urgency, you push him or her into action. This is why commercials love to declare, "Time is running out! Get your order in within the next twenty minutes and you get free shipping! But this won't last long!" These silly ads are actually very clever because they make people feel like they need to make a purchase now, or else they will miss out on a deal forever. You can persuade people to take action or buy something from you by using urgency as well.

Offer an Incentive

People are mainly driven by two things: money and social interaction. You can offer someone a social or economic incentive to get them to agree to something. You basically provide the promise of a reward, and people are likely to act to get that reward.

Conditioning

Similar to offering an incentive, conditioning is when you train someone to associate a stimulus or reward with doing what you want. If you have to deal with a difficult person often, you can condition that person to do what you want and stop making your life difficult. You can play the person's favorite music or offer the person a snack whenever he or she engages in a behavior that you can condone. Soon, the person will subconsciously associate a rewarding experience with pleasing you. He or she will start to work to please you in response to the conditioning stimulus, such as the sound of his or her favorite song. It may take a few exposures, but conditioning is quite powerful. You can essentially train people to stop being difficult using conditioning.

Chapter 8: When to Walk Away

Not all relationships are worth keeping. Not all people are worth fighting for. If someone adds more difficulty to your life than benefit, you should seriously reevaluate the relationship. Is someone really worth so much stress and unhappiness?

There comes a point when it is acceptable and even expected for you to walk away from people that bring you down. Some people are just difficult, but they are still lovable. They still treat you well and offer your life value. People who pose difficulties without adding value to your life are simply a drain on your energy, happiness, and life resources. They tax your emotions and ruin your peace. They may even hurt you. Why put up with these people any longer?

You don't have to take a lot of nonsense and rudeness from anyone. Standing up for yourself does not make you a bad person. People who love you may hurt you occasionally. It is a fact of life. But people who really do care about you will try to avoid hurting you as much as they can. If someone continually hurts you by lying to you or otherwise disrespecting you, then he or she certainly does not care about your feelings. You are more like a pawn to be used for some sort of end for this person, rather than a loved one. You deserve better treatment, especially from those that you look to as loved ones.

People need to treat you with a certain level of respect if they want to be with you or exist in your life. They need to offer some sort of value to your life, not just hurt and emotional exhaustion. Sometimes, people think that they can get away with pushing you around. It is important for you to set boundaries to let people know that they cannot treat you certain ways. The best way to set boundaries is to staunchly tell people no when they try to do things that you don't like. For instance, it is perfectly acceptable for you to ask people to take their shoes off when they enter your house. Practice asking people to do things like take off their shoes without apology to teach people that you have expectations for certain behavior and you are not afraid to say no or demand what you really want.

Offer people consequences for treating you badly and violating your boundaries. The consequence of a first transgression is a warning: Do not treat me this way ever again. You must stop worrying about how much people will get angry with you when you stand up for yourself. Most people will be surprised when you set boundaries and they will stand down. The people who do not grow respect for you are the people that do not need to be in your life. The consequence for a second transgression is cutting off the relationship. You do not need people who blatantly disrespect you and your boundaries in your life.

When people see that you do not tolerate mistreatment and that you offer very real consequences for transgressions and disrespect, they will be more likely to respect you. They will not want to test your boundaries. Most people will respond well to you if you set up firm boundaries. You may fear that people will start to hate you if you become firmer. But the opposite is usually true. People will like you more and treat you better as they start to respect you. Standing up for yourself usually helps make people less difficult.

But there are always some people who will test your boundaries and laugh at the consequence that you offer. These people may even try to intimidate you into giving up on your self-respecting boundaries. Family is especially bad at this, because family is used to being in control. They will not appreciate your new efforts to set boundaries, especially if you have not stood up for yourself in the past. Do not let these people make you waver in your resolve. Stand up for yourself. Chew people out for disrespecting you and do not be afraid to walk away from disrespectful relationships.

You should carefully consider all of your relationships. How do certain people make you feel? If you find that a certain person just makes you feel awful more than he or she makes you feel good, you should consider whether the relationship is worth salvaging. Some people, such as spouses or family members, are worth fighting for. You should focus on improving the relationship, rather than scrapping it. But some people are not worth any effort on your part at all. These are the people who offer no value to your life. These people do not pay your bills or love you or have any history with you. You should not give them the time of day. They are literally a burden, not an asset. They offer nothing to you so don't worry so much about their opinions. Definitely don't keep tolerating the difficulties that they create in your life.

Also look at the kinds of difficulties that people cause you. When someone is causing difficulty, ask yourself, Is this just an inconvenience, or is it a truly unnecessary drama? Sometimes, you have to tolerate unpleasant interactions with certain people for a reason. But unreasonable drama that causes you trouble for no good reason is useless. You have enough to deal with in your life. You do not have to tolerate more stress that does not serve you any good, valuable purpose.

When you leave a difficult person behind in your past, you can cut ties cleanly. You can say that you are done and you can state exactly why.

Be prepared for a fight or hurt feelings, however.

Sometimes it easier to simply put distance

between yourself and someone else. Start to

avoid him or her. Only tell him or her how you

feel if he or she asks. You do not owe anyone an

explanation for your actions and you do not have

to put up with a fight when you sever ties with

someone.

Conclusion

Difficult people of all kinds are inevitable in life. You will run into people who behave in ways that do not align with your intents and goals. These people seem determined to make your life harder, but in reality, their behavior is probably not aimed directly at you. You can make the best of these situations and actually get along better with difficult people.

It is important to understand that all people are different. What you want is probably never going to match what someone else wants. Misaligned goals and other differences often lead to the conflict that makes human interaction difficult. Overcoming differences requires patience and good communication.

Sometimes, people act difficult for reasons that have nothing to do with you. You need to stop taking the difficult behavior of others so personally. Try to be more empathetic and improve communication. Approach difficult people as a challenge to be overcome. Find the source of their difficult behavior, and work with people to find an ideal solution for it.

Other times, people act difficult because they are envious of you or angry with you. Handling the emotions of other people that are directed at you can be nerve-wracking. You may have to swallow your pride and apologize to someone for a transgression. Alternatively, you can just walk away and not deal with the drama at all.

Loved ones are often the most difficult people of all. Handling fights, deception, manipulation, and other issues with loved ones can be very hard. It can also be very hurtful. You must remember to remain caring and loving with your loved ones as you try to find out why they are being so difficult. Work with them to help heal the behavior, rather than fight with them.

You really can safely and gently deal with difficult people while avoiding drama and fights. There are ways to maturely address the issues you have with others without leading to further conflict. You will be surprised how well people respond to you if you make an effort to reach an agreeable solution with them.

However, sometimes you just have to walk away from some people. You cannot reasonably tolerate people who are more difficult to deal with than they are worth. You have the right to avoid unhappiness and drama in your life, but some people just bring emotional turmoil and conflict along with them wherever they go. You must clear useless baggage from your life and surround yourself with enjoyable, positive people. Some people offer no value to your life, so cut them off.

You cannot change difficult people. But you can change yourself. Changing your attitude and your reactions toward difficult people can drastically change your interpersonal interactions. You may suddenly find yourself encountering fewer difficult interactions and fewer difficult people as you become more understanding and more communicative.

Using the tips in this book can help you unlock a new level of peace and ease in your life as you end difficult conflicts with other people. You can use the tips contained in these pages to learn how to deal with different types of difficult people in more effective manners. You can also use this book as a guide on how to achieve better communication and conflict resolution skills. From walking away to becoming a better communicator, this book has all sorts of advice that you need to start solving the problems that you run into with more difficult people.

Your life will be much easier if you learn to stop inadvertently causing conflict and judging people. You will feel better if you stop taking difficult behavior personally. You can smooth out the bumps in your life significantly just by changing your own behavior. You cannot reasonably change others, and if you try, you will be frustrated and disappointed. But if you change your own behavior, you will find that others will respond to you differently. You can influence them to behave differently. You hold the power to turn difficult people and situations around fast, and this book will help you unlock that power.

Thanks for reading!

Other great books by Madison Taylor on Kindle, paperback and audio

Rejection Proof Therapy 101: How To Overcome, Deal With And Heal Yourself From Rejection

Cognitive Behavioral Therapy For Beginners: How To Use CBT To Overcome Anxieties, Phobias, Addictions, Depression, Negative Thoughts, And Other Problematic Disorders

Forbidden Psychology 101: The Cool Stuff They Didn't Teach You About In School

Escaping the Introvert World: The Introvert's Guide To Overcoming Shyness, Social Anxiety, And Fear To Thrive In An Extrovert World

NLP For Beginners: Learn the Secrets of Self Mastery, Developing Magnetic Influence and Reaching Your Goals Using Neuro-Linguistic Programming

Depression Proof Yourself: How To Avoid And Overcome Being Depressed

Love Thyself: The First Commandment to Raising your Self Esteem, Boosting your Self-Confidence, and Increasing your Happiness

The Art of Decision Making: How to Make Better Choices in Love, Life, and Work

The Dark Science of Psychological Warfare: How To Always Keep The Upper Hand On Anyone Psychologically

Staying Focused: How to Effectively Eliminate the Weapons of Mass Distraction

Turbo Charged NLP: A New and Improved Way of Taking Self Mastery, Influence, and Neuro-linguistic Programming to the Next Level

The Art of Deception: How To Master And Use Subterfuge On Anyone